MORE
rareAIR

I'M BACK!

TEXT BY MICHAEL JORDAN

PHOTOGRAPHS BY WALTER IOOSS, JR.

EDITED BY MARK VANCIL

CollinsPublishersSanFrancisco

Published Internationally by HarperCollins*Publishers*

Produced by
Rare Air, Ltd.
A Mark Vancil Company

Photography by
Walter Iooss, Jr.

Edited by
Mark Vancil

Designed by
Greg Niedbala

McMillan Associates
130 Washington Street
West Dundee, Illinois 60118

Special Thanks to:
Laura Sadovi-Vancil, Eva, Christian and
Bjorn Iooss, Jacqueline, Susan and
Loren Vancil, Jane and Justin Haka,
Bill Mabel, Paul Sheridan and David Falk

At McMillan Associates:
Anne McMillan

At the NBA:
Frank Fochetta and Brian McIntyre

With the Chicago Bulls:
Phil Jackson, Tim Hallam, Chip Schaefer
and John Ligmanowski

First published 1995 by
Collins Publishers San Francisco
Some of this material previously appeared
in RareAir, originally published in 1993
Published Internationally by
HarperCollins Publishers

Collins Publishers San Francisco books may be
purchased for educational, business, or sales
promotion use. For information, please call or
write: Special Markets Department, Harper
Collins Publishers, 10 E. 53rd Street, New York,
New York 10022.

Library of Congress Cataloging-in-
Publication Data

Jordan, Michael, 1963-
I'm back!: more rare air/text by Michael Jordan.
photographs by Walter Iooss, Jr.:
edited by Mark Vancil.
p. cm.
Updated version of: RareAir. 1993.
ISBN 0-00-649153-7
    1. Jordan, Michael, 1963- Pictorial works.
    2. Basketball players—United States—
      Biography.
    I. Iooss, Walter.
    II. Vancil, Mark, 1958-.
    III. Jordan, Michael, 1963- Rare air.
    IV. Title.
GV884.J64S3 1995
796.323′092—DC20   95-9364
                                         CIP

Printed in the United States of America
10 9 8 7 6 5 4 3 2 1

FOR JUANITA, JEFFREY, MARCUS AND JASMINE.

IN MEMORY OF MY FATHER, JAMES.

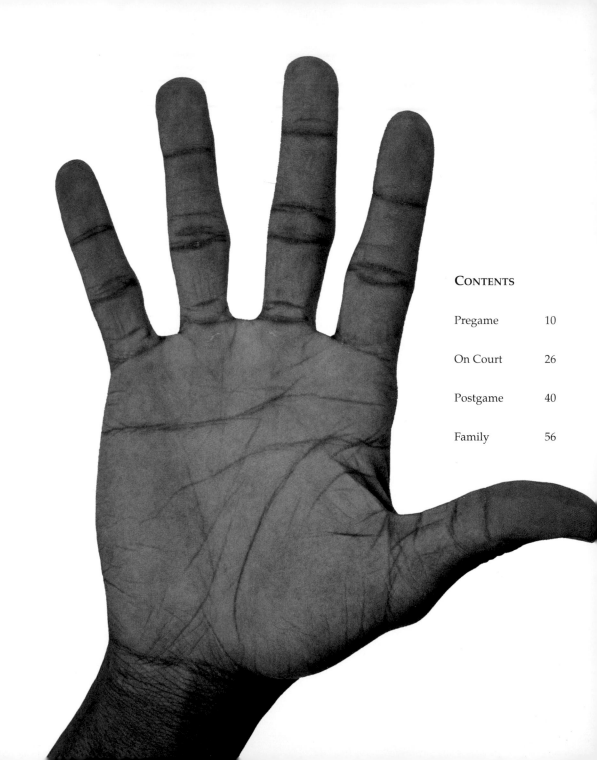

CONTENTS

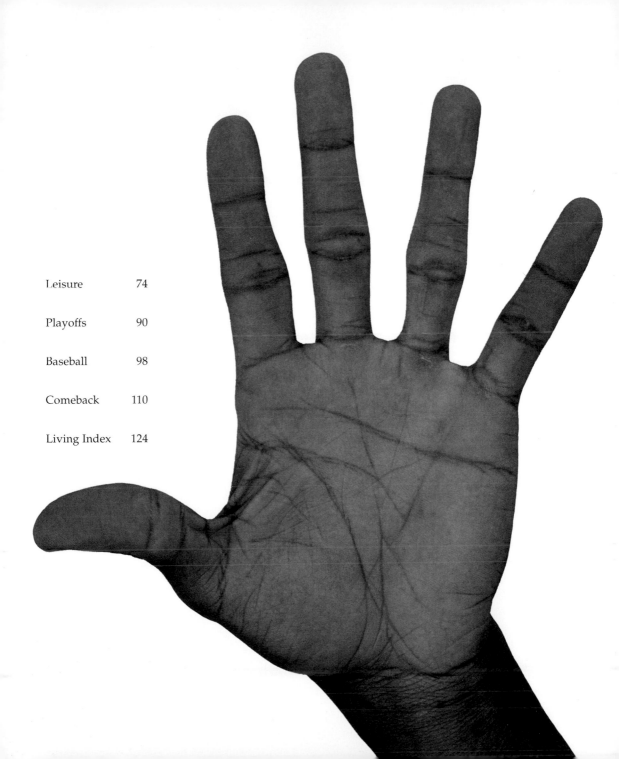

I WANT THEM TO KNOW THE WHOLE EXPERIENCE IS REAL.

I'VE NEVER REALLY BEEN A VOCAL KIND OF GUY. My leadership, in practice or games, has always come from the way I approach the game and the way I play once I step onto the court. I try not to be negative, especially in practice. Instead, I try to make practice as competitive as possible, so hopefully, other guys will feed off me.

Now, I can't say, 'OK, you guys practice your behinds off because that's why we're here and we need it.' I don't do that. I go out and do my job and I do it in a very competitive way. If you don't bring your level up to compete with me then I'm going to completely dominate you, and I'm going to talk trash to you and about you while I'm dominating. That's my way of getting my teammates to elevate their game.

Sometimes I try to raise the level of competition in practice by talking trash to them. Other times the competitive level rises naturally when Phil changes up the rotations so that I'm playing opposite Scottie Pippen, or my group is working against some of the other starters. It becomes a challenge and that's exactly how I approach the situation.

And there are times when the first team feels like we need to work on a specific part of our game. When that happens, the competitive level has to be high. It's a matter of talking trash to the second team or doing whatever is necessary to test their heart and drive to see if they want to compete.

Personally, I can't take it easy in practices and then expect myself to just turn it on in the games. I have to turn it on in practice if it's going to be there in games. That's why I've never complained about practices. But if you're just going to show up and go through the motions, then I'd rather not play at all. I saw some Dream Teamers dog it in practice before the Olympics. I looked at them and I knew that's what separates me from them. I would never say that I'm better, but I knew I would be confident when I played against those guys because my work ethic is better.

I guess my appetite for practice comes from my years at the University of North Carolina. Coach Smith used to make practices so competitive that you had to raise your level of play. You could win points in practice. I wouldn't call it favoritism, but you knew that if you went all out all the time, you could get more playing time and respect. So that's why I approach practice as a kind of proving ground.

That's especially true with rookies or guys that are traded to the Bulls. Rookies are fun because I always feel that I have to prove myself to them. They've probably seen me on television, read about me in newspapers and they might think they know what I'm all about or what it's like to play against me. But I feel like I have a reputation to defend and I'm going to show them that I live up to that reputation. I want them to know that what they heard isn't just gossip or rumors. I want them to know that it all comes from hard work. So when they come into a Chicago Bulls camp, they're going to see it all and I'm going to find out what they have and whether they can compete with me.

It's the same thing when a veteran comes to our team. Let's say Rodney McCray gets traded to the Bulls. I feel that if I'm considered one of the best players in the game, then I have to prove there is a reason for that. And the reason that I'm at that level is because I practice harder and do all the necessary things to put myself at that level. I want them to know that. Maybe they came from a team that had a star as well. But there is a difference. Maybe their star didn't work as hard or approach every practice and game the way I do. I want to prove to them that, 'Hey, I deserve what I get.' I want them to know I don't take all kinds of days off or think of myself as a prima donna. I want them to see how hard I work to be at this level. I want them to know the whole experience is real.

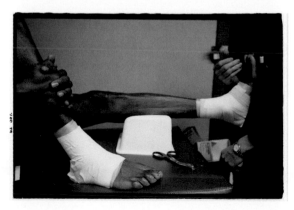

My ritual is the same before every game. My pregame meal is steak and potatoes or steak and french fries. I don't screw around with that because I know that if I get the steak and potatoes, the protein is going to be there whenever I need to reach down, particularly in the third or fourth quarter. That's just how much I'm in tune with my body.

People say I eat like a bird and that's true. Birds eat just enough to fly. All those birds that eat a lot end up getting eaten themselves. Turkeys, chickens. They can't fly. The others eat just enough to get by, just enough to fly. That's how I am.

I already have my stuff together by the time I eat, which is about three hours before the game. Maybe I play cards with the guys, or watch a movie on television, but all day I'm going back and forth between thinking about those things and thinking about the game. That's part of the nervousness. Are we going to have a big game or a little game? I start picturing the way I want to play. Naturally, I'm envisioning us winning no matter how I play. I can envision a big game for myself, but I can't guarantee it's going to happen.

When I do envision a big game, I usually go out and play passively at the beginning. I let the game come to me. It's very important that I don't go try to make it happen. Some days I just feel it. When I scored 54 points against New York or 55 points against Phoenix, I knew that day I was going to have a good game. I had a feeling that I would. But it isn't like I came out of the box scoring 30 points in the first quarter. I came out and got maybe 10 or 12. Then maybe 8 more in the second quarter. And then in the second half, when I have the confidence that, 'Hey, I can throw this big number at them,' that's when I can score 20 or 25 points in a quarter. Because then I've found the rhythm of the game.

I CONSIDER PHIL JACKSON TO BE THE DEAN SMITH OF THE PROFESSIONAL GAME. Coach Smith really cares about his players at the University of North Carolina. Phil's the same way with the Bulls. He has his own idiosyncrasies and he employs psychological warfare to make you think about your mistakes or to understand the team concept. But I respect that, because he's able to do it on a professional level where he has to blend egos together so that they have the same team focus. He's got a special talent for that. Coach Smith does as well.

Away from the game, I don't know him that well. I think he has some great values in terms of how to approach life, and what you should get out of life relative to your needs and desires. Being around him, you can only learn to be a better basketball player as well as a better person. You can sense that he had good parental guidance growing up in terms of right and wrong, being his own man and holding strongly to his beliefs.

He does give me some responsibility about decisions as they relate to the team. He lets me use my judgment. If he feels he must correct me or say something that's in the best interest of the team, I can accept it and he knows that. I think we have a very good relationship. A lot of times you see egos clashing between coaches and their star players. But I respect any criticism he might give me. I don't discredit or challenge it. I still feel he's the coach and I'm the player.

We can talk about anything that we might disagree about. Coach Smith was a little different because at the time I was under his wing, I was very intimidated by him. Whatever he said, I readily accepted. But with Phil, he gives you a little more room to be your own man, to be independent and to make decisions that you feel are in the best interest of the team. A lot of coaches won't do that.

I WEAR A DIFFERENT PAIR OF SHOES EVERY NIGHT. It's funny because when I explain why I do that, everyone can relate. Anybody that goes out and buys something new, let's say a new pair of shoes or a new suit, you feel good about it. I wanted to feel that way every game. You feel energized, you feel a little better about yourself. That's why I started doing it. I didn't do that my first year. But as I started putting on a new pair of shoes I felt like, 'I'm walking out there with my own shoes and I'm happy as hell.'

I always lace up my own shoes, too. I take my time because I want them to be laced a certain way and it's something that keeps me busy. But when I'm ready, there's no more fooling around. Let's go. As far as the shoes go, I give them away unless it's a memorable game. I have the shoes from the 69-point game against Cleveland in 1990. The 63-point game against Boston in the 1986 playoffs, I have those too. And I've kept my shoes from every championship game.

Two things never change: my pregame meal and my Carolina blue shorts. I wear my Carolina shorts every game, every day. Every single day of my life since I left college. I just feel comfortable with them on. That's where it all started for me. As long as I have these shorts on, and I have them on whether I'm playing a game or wearing a suit, I feel confident. That whole memory keeps me going. That differentiates me from other players, I think. That was the foundation of my game, of my career.

I still get chills when I hear the introductions, particularly at Chicago Stadium. That's the respect the fans are giving you. I hear it. I know there are people there. I hear the yelling. But I don't hear anything outside of that.

I don't totally focus until game time. I'm one of those guys that if you walk into the locker room before the game, you would probably see me fooling around and telling jokes. But 15 minutes later, you can't say a word to me.

Other than the Carolina shorts, the only superstition I have is that I have to get my ankles taped last. I'm the last to get dressed. My game face could be any face. I could laugh, anything. My game face has many looks.

THE FIRST THING I DO WHEN I WALK ONTO THE COURT IS TO FIND MY WIFE OR FAMILY IF THEY ARE COMING TO THE GAME. I can't relax and play the game until I find out where they are sitting and I know that they've arrived safely.

If my wife isn't there when the game starts, then she knows I'm going to be upset when I get into the car after the game. I don't know what might have happened. I need her to be there when the game starts because I need to be at ease with myself. That's why I look up into the stands. There have been times when my wife or parents weren't there when the game started and I ended up looking around while I was on the floor until they arrived. They know that the one thing I must know before I can play the game is that everyone arrived safely. My mind must be at ease about those things before I can work. That's just my nature.

IF YOU'RE NOT GOING TO COMPETE, THEN I'LL DOMINATE YOU.

WHEN I STEP ONTO THE COURT, I'M READY TO PLAY. And if you're playing against me, then you'd better be ready, too. If you're not going to compete, then I'll dominate you. If it's going to be, 'I'll let you score and you let me score,' then no thanks. It's not good basketball. Basketball is about competition. That's the essence of the game. If you're letting somebody score on you and he's letting you score on him, like an all-star game or something like that, then that's not competing. Then it's just a show, an exhibition with everybody acting like they're playing. If that's the case, I'd rather not play.

That's just my nature and the nature of my preparation. That's why when I need to dig deep inside myself, I can do that because I've done it before and it's part of my preparation. I've been to that place before. I know where it's at, how to get there and what it feels like to go deep inside for that extra push or pull I might need. A lot of other guys, when they start digging deep, they say to themselves, 'Hey, I don't need this. It's only a game.' That drives me nuts. I can't play with anybody like that. Yes, it's a game, but the object of the game is to win. Now I know a lot of people might approach it another way. They might think, 'It is only a game and you are supposed to have fun, so you shouldn't make a game larger than life.' I don't agree with that. If I'm going to play, then when I walk in between those white lines,

I'm going to play to win. I'm not out there just to be playing. That's just not me. That's not my attitude.

And that's why I've adjusted my game over the years. It isn't that I've totally changed my game. It's that I'm willing to take what the defense gives me and I'm willing to do what's necessary to excel at what they are forcing me to do. Most teams now force me to shoot the outside shot. I'm telling them, 'I can shoot that shot and I can be just as effective and just as big a threat.' I don't want anyone to feel that I have a weakness. My attitude is, if you push me toward something that you think is a weakness, then I will turn that perceived weakness into a strength. So now you're making me do something that I'm comfortable doing. Not only have I added to my weapons, but I've improved upon all of them in the process.

The real adjustment, though, came after the 1986-87 season when I averaged 37.1 points a game. A lot of those points came off drives to the basket. People saw that I could be a scoring machine if they just tried to cut me off or play me one-on-one. They knew my skills were too good for that type of defense. So teams started making adjustments, figuring the weakest part of my game was my outside shot. Most teams decided that they would rather see me shoot from the perimeter than let me get into the paint. So I had to adjust.

WHEN I'M PLAYING AGAINST SCORERS, PLAYERS LIKE REGGIE
MILLER, CLYDE DREXLER AND JOE DUMARS, I'M ENVISIONING
THEIR TENDENCIES BEFORE THE GAME. Should I attack him
offensively early so that he's on the defensive for the
rest of the game? There are different ways I have to
approach players like that because I have to stop them
as well as score on them. Sometimes, doing one can
impact the other.

I've played Clyde so much that I know he's dangerous if
he can't score early. But he's not dangerous when he
comes out shooting and scoring. Isn't that wild? If he
hits his first five shots, it's not as much of a problem for
me because he'll shoot himself out of the game. Now if
Joe Dumars hits his first five shots, then I'm in big trouble. He knows how to feed off the kind of confidence
you get from a good start. Clyde, on the other hand,
sometimes seems like he gets overconfident, and he
might start taking all kinds of shots.

But Dumars, he's going to sit back and let the game come to him because he's in a rhythm and he's going to make you work. Miller is the same way because he feeds off that energy. If he makes his first five shots, he starts to talk trash and he's into the game. He gets more intense, more focused. Those are three different people and three different ways I have to play them.

Defensively, I'm like everyone else. I'm guessing, basically. When I'm at my best offensively, I know I can dictate what I want to do. Defensively, I can dictate some things, but not nearly as much as I can offensively. That's just the nature of the game.

But I think I'm the best at this particular time because I play both ends of the court. The best ever? I can't say that. But I play both ends. And I do a lot of things that go unnoticed. How do I compare to others? I don't know. I just think that I do a lot more than they do.

I ALWAYS FELT I COULD SHOOT. When I came out of college everyone said, 'He can't shoot the jumper.' I never had to. I could penetrate zones in college. And teams played me one-on-one at North Carolina. They never double-teamed me. I always had a quick enough first step to get to the hole. I never looked to be aggressive offensively in college because I was playing in a system and I was learning the game.

That was the education I got from Dean Smith. Coming out of high school, I had all the ability in the world but I didn't know the game. Dean taught me the game, when to apply speed, how to use your quickness, when to use that first step, or how to apply certain skills in certain situations. I gained all that knowledge so that when I got to the pros, it was just a matter of applying the information.

A lot of people say Dean Smith held me to under 20 points a game. Dean Smith gave me the knowledge to score 37 points a game and that's something people don't understand.

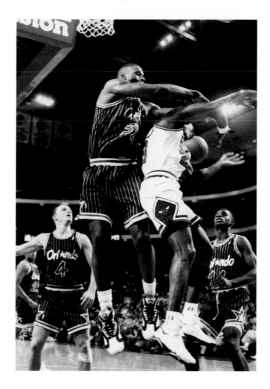

A LOT OF PEOPLE ASK ME HOW I APPROACH SCORING. Scoring is scoring. If I want to average 32 points a game, I can do that easily. It's just eight, eight, eight, eight. No problem. I can do that anytime. That's not being cocky. That's confidence. I know the flow of the game, how many shots I'm going to get. It's no problem because I'm so in tune with my skills and the system I'm involved with.

I WAS THE KIND OF GUY IN SCHOOL THAT IF I HAD A TERM PAPER TO DO, I'D WAIT UNTIL THE VERY LAST MINUTE. The first time you're able to come through in that situation then you think you can do it all the time. Now relate that to basketball. The first time you hit a jump shot with no time on the clock, you can always go back to that moment. You have the confidence because you've done it before.

I wasn't afraid to take a big shot in the professional ranks because I had made one when I was a snotty-nosed kid in 1982 to beat Georgetown. That's why I say that my career really started when I made that shot. I was fearless after that. I had gone through every test there was and I had come out on top. What can be any more pressure than hitting the game-winning shot for your team in an NCAA title game as a freshman?

That started my career. Why? Because I had that confidence. No one could take that away from me. I was in that situation and I came through. Now when I get in that situation, I don't weigh the negatives and positives and hope the positives win. I just go back to my past successes, step forward and respond. That's why your great players, guys like Jerry West, make great plays in clutch situations consistently. They have something to compare it to whenever the situation presents itself. They can accept the consequences because they've done it before. It takes talent, but it takes guts. Not everybody has them. Where does it come from? I don't know. But I think it must come from your work ethic.

You do it on smaller scales until you build up to an NBA championship game. You do it in Little League when your team needs a home run and pow, you knock it out of the damn park. Then in high school you need a basket to win the Christmas championship and pow, there it is. Then you move up to college. Each level, the confidence grows stronger and stronger until you get to the highest level, where I am now, and you're thinking, 'Give me the ball. I'll shoot it. No problem.' If you make the shot, then everybody will be shaking your hand. If you miss, you've done it before,

IF I WAS LOOKING FOR PLAYERS I WOULD WANT AROUND ME, I'D LOOK FOR QUICKNESS, HEART, AND STRONG FUNDAMENTALS. Ability comes last. If you've got a good mind for the game, you can overcome the lack of ability in certain areas.

Look at Larry Bird. He's a prime example. He was slow. He couldn't jump that well. He had good hands, good ball handling and shooting skills. But he was very smart. He could outthink his opponents and he had a big heart.

Heart is probably the biggest key to success in basketball at this level. There are a lot of players who pass through the NBA with the ability, but they don't have the heart or the intelligence to get the job done. That's the divider, always has been.

Give me four guys of average ability with strong fundamentals and big hearts and I'll take my chances every time. Big games come down to those two things. The team that executes is usually the team that reaches inside for that little extra. I want those kinds of guys with me.

BASKETBALL ISN'T MY JOB.

BASKETBALL ISN'T MY JOB. For me, my job begins the moment I walk off the floor. It's everything that surrounds the actual playing of the games. My job is being a product endorser, an employee of the Chicago Bulls, trying to live up to the expectations of others, dealing with the media. That's my job.

The media part of that has never been very difficult for me, though. I like people. That's just my personality. I just believe that if you treat them with respect, then they will respect you. That's not always true, as I've found out. But for the most part, I try to do that because I genuinely like some of the reporters I deal with. Some of them are very honest. So I don't want to deprive them of something they might need to perform their jobs. I think I owe that respect to them. But, as of late, I don't think I have been given the same kind of respect in return.

I knew that, at some point in time, people were going to start taking shots at me. When you're on top, some people want to knock you down. I can accept that. But I never thought that it would be someone that I knew, someone that I had spent time with and someone that I had been frank with on a lot of subjects.

That's what bothered me most about the book *The Jordan Rules*. There was never any confrontation, nothing to make me aware of what was going on. That was just selfishness on the part of the writer. If that person was the friend he pretended he was, then why not at least let me know what you're doing behind the scenes? Instead he kept it under wraps and then bam, it hits the papers. I felt betrayed.

I think I'm a good judge of character. But I've been burned a couple times now by people that I've let into my inner circle and that's a scary situation. The way I look at it, I was just wrong about those particular people.

There are a lot of people who say they would like to be Michael Jordan for a day or a week or a month. But that's not fair. You've got to do it

three, four, five years and see everything build to the point where your privacy has disappeared and your life, virtually every moment of your life, is being monitored. Sure, for a day, a week, or maybe even a month, it might be fun. You might get a free meal somewhere or have the opportunity to drive different cars. But wait until someone steals your license plates off your car, every car, every other week.

Play an NBA game, rush to get on a plane, fly for an hour or two and then at 3 o'clock in the morning, try to get to your room with 20 or 30 people yelling for an autograph. Either way you lose. Your knees hurt, your back aches, your whole body's sore, and you have practice in six hours. Even if I say, 'I'm sorry, but I'm really tired,' they don't understand.

I'm not complaining. It's just that the demands aren't always apparent to others. The idea of being a role model is part of what I consider my job. You are asked to be the purest of the pure. But there isn't anyone on earth like that. I try to live up to that ideal as much as possible by doing what's right. That's just human nature. But when you ask someone to be a role model, you have to understand that person is human just like you are. That person goes to the bathroom, he gets a cold, his nose bleeds.

No matter how hard I try, I'm never going to be the perfect person. The one time I tell somebody that I'm tired and that I don't want to sign another autograph, that person gets a whole different feeling about Michael Jordan. So my job really never ends. Every day I interact with people and I have to be positive. I have to smile. I have to be in a good mood. Because when I don't, someone could have a negative feeling about who or what I am. And I don't want someone to get the wrong impression of what kind of person I am. I don't want people to feel that way about me.

I REALLY CAN'T GET A SENSE OF WHO I AM OR WHETHER I'M AS FAMOUS AS PEOPLE SAY. Maybe that's one of the reasons I'm the person that I am. I don't know how I'm supposed to act. I can only be the person that I am naturally.

I know some people act completely different because of their fame or celebrity status, but I couldn't be something else. My personality, the way I was raised, wouldn't allow me to change just because of what someone might think of me.

Really, I can't envision myself on everybody's wall and inside people's houses. I suppose that's happened. But I can't let myself get to the point of accepting that and then thinking I'm something or someone that I've never been. I don't think my ego will let me get to that point. I don't consider myself better than the next man. I'm just fortunate that I have a little more than that person.

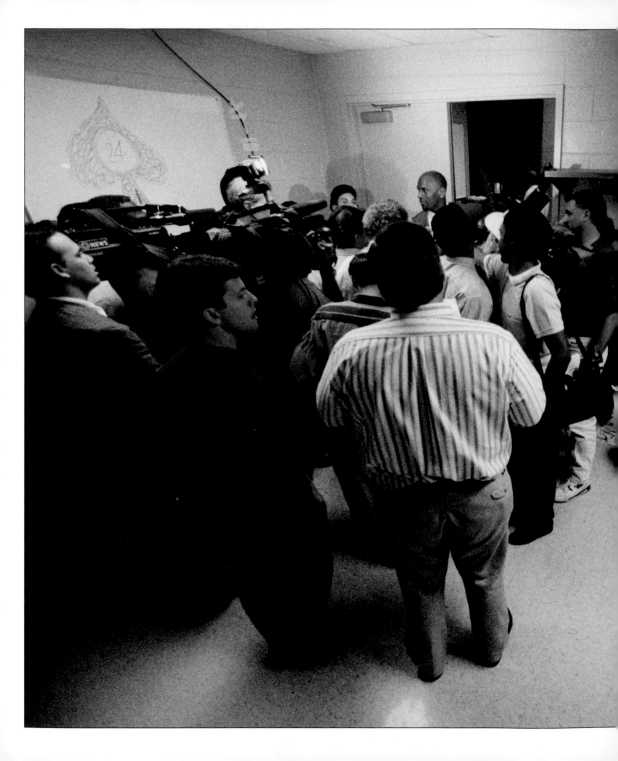

I'M VERY CONSCIOUS OF THINGS THAT
ARE SAID ABOUT OUR TEAM, PARTICU-
LARLY AS IT RELATES TO ME AND THE
EMPHASIS THAT OTHERS PUT ON ME.
Like people calling us 'Michael
Jordan and the Jordanaires.' If I was
one of the so-called Jordanaires, that
would hurt.

I understand my role. I know what
my contributions are to this team
and I think everyone else understands too. It's not hard to accept
that role because I know it's a major
role. I know what I have to do for
our team. But I also know this is a
team, and that regardless of my
stature, I'm part of that team.

WHEN I WAS A KID, I NEVER ASKED FOR ONE AUTOGRAPH. What can a name on a piece of paper do for me? Nothing. Other people can inspire me but I never thought a name on a piece of paper would do that. Even though I do sign, I just can't see myself ever asking for an autograph. I guess I'm self-confident enough that I don't need an autograph to motivate me to be a better person or to make me feel better about myself. Some people do though and I don't fault those people. But me, I've always had so much self-confidence that a name on a piece of paper isn't going to mean anything.

I can't even think of anyone I idolized when I was growing up or someone whose signature I would have wanted. I remember seeing David Thompson once from a distance. I was observing him and I was curious about seeing him in person because he was one of the greatest basketball players ever. But to go up to him and invade his space and time — I would have felt like an idiot to do that. Now I'm not saying these people asking for autographs are idiots. But that's the way I would have felt about myself. I couldn't do that.

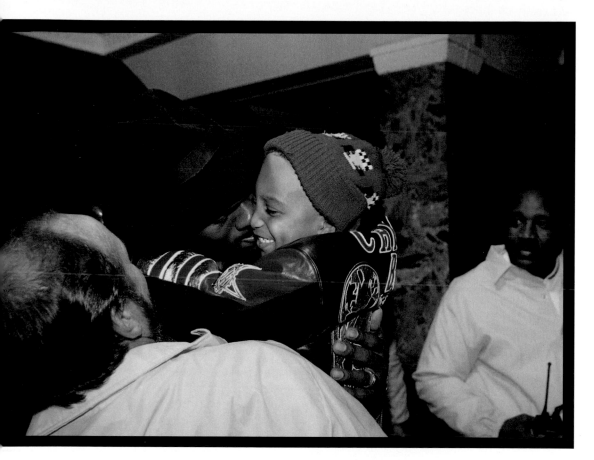

My life has been an education. You can't teach what I'm learning or what I'm going through. There are no classes to prepare you, no books to read or lessons to study. I had a very good foundation, thanks to my schooling and my parents, but I had to learn about this life.

I tell my wife all the time that what I do for a living is a game. It's a game on the basketball court and it's a game off the court. It's knowing when to say, 'Yes, sir,' and when to say, 'No, sir.' I want people to appreciate what I do and the kind of person I am. I want them to see me as a positive person. But you have to understand that for some people it really is nothing more than a game. Because there are a lot of games they are trying to play with you.

Like my Wheaties deal. They wanted to interview me before signing me to endorse the product. Fine. So they ask me if I eat Wheaties. I could have easily lied. But I thought, why lie? So I told them the truth. I told them I had never eaten Wheaties and that I didn't know whether I'd even like Wheaties. I mean, we used to eat some kind of wheat puffs when I was growing up. They came in a huge bag. I don't even know if they had a brand name. We had five kids in the family. We couldn't afford Wheaties. Now if I would have lied about that, would they have still signed me? I don't know. But I didn't want them to think I was lying, so I told the truth.

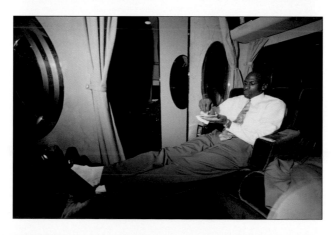

IT'S EASIER FOR ME TO GET READY FOR A GAME ON THE ROAD BECAUSE YOU'RE EXPECTED TO LOSE WHEN YOU PLAY AWAY FROM HOME. That's a challenge for me right there and that perks up my competitive juices. I don't want to go out when I'm on the road because I'm focusing on what we have to do. I don't feel like mingling with people who would rather watch me lose. That's just part of the competitive attitude I have.

I don't mind administering machines or medicines to my body if it gets me ready to play. But I won't take drugs. And I won't take shots to cover the pain. I'll do all the necessary work to help the healing process. I want to be there at game time so I'll do whatever else it takes to get myself ready.

My feet take a beating, though. Because my style of play is so much stopping and cutting, it tears up my feet. If anything happens to my feet, I can't go.

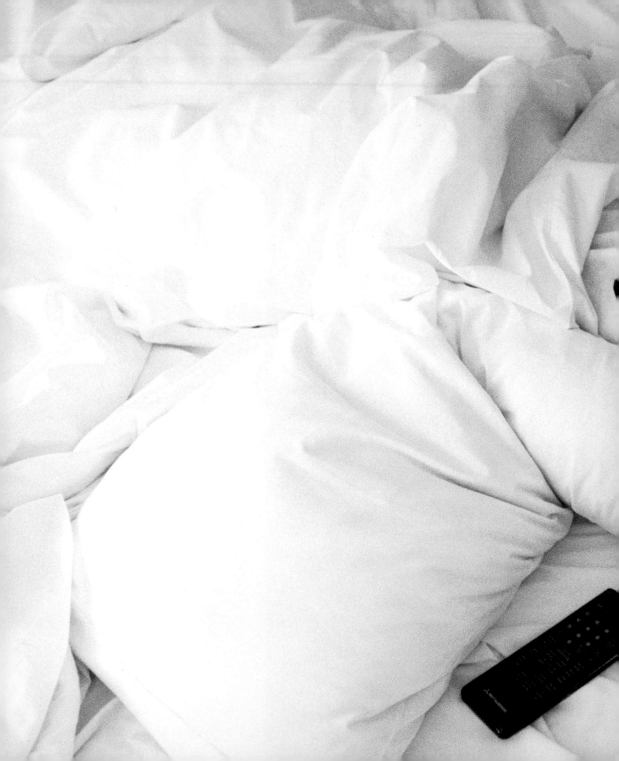

I DO MISS ALL THE TIME THAT I'M NOT THERE.

SOMETIMES I WONDER WHAT IT WOULD BE LIKE NOT TO BE MICHAEL JORDAN. Or to be Michael Jordan, but to be just like everyone else who has a family and is able to do family things.

My perfect day? I would get up in the morning and go to a pancake house with my wife and kids and have breakfast. If it was summertime, I'd say, 'Let's go to Great America.' I haven't been to an amusement park since I was 12 or 13 myself. I can't go. I can, but I don't want to go through the whole spectacle. It's not fair to the children.

So I would take them to an amusement park. Then I'd take the family to lunch, maybe at McDonald's or Hardee's. Then maybe we'd go ride bicycles through the neighborhood without someone following me in a car or running alongside. Then at night I'd go for a walk. Just a walk with my wife and kids. And then maybe I'd go to a movie. That would be my day. That would be my perfect day.

I know all of this is hard on my children. I try to provide a normal life for them. But right now I can't be there for Little League practice. I can't be there to help them with their homework. I want to do those things. My wife, Juanita, is really my contact with the children. She takes them to the dentist, takes them to the doctor. I'm not in tune with those things until my wife tells me about them. It's the same with school. That's why I think the role of the mother is overlooked in our society. It's critical, especially in our case.

That's why I thank my wife, because she has to take care of everything from their education to teaching them right from wrong. Once I get away from basketball, I'll get more in tune with all the details of their lives. I realize that, but it's still hard knowing time is passing and I'm not there to see all the changes.

Right now I think it's harder on the boys. It's always, 'Let's go play basketball, Daddy. Let's go play baseball, Daddy.' I'm starting to get more of that now. I do a lot when I'm home, but I just miss so much because of my schedule.

Jeffrey is the oldest and he understands that I'm a special person because all his friends tell him. The younger kids communicate so much that he's starting to understand that I'm different. They'll tell him, 'Oh, your dad is a big star. He plays for the Bulls. He was the Most Valuable Player in the NBA Finals.' They tell him all that stuff. So Jeffrey is starting to comprehend a little more about my life. Marcus? He couldn't care less right now. He's at that age that he doesn't really care what I do.

But children are so rewarding. To have kids, that makes it easy to get through any problem. I find myself looking at my children, just watching them and realizing how fortunate I am. Everything I've done on the basketball court, in business, nothing compares to having them. And I'm sure other people feel the same way about their kids.

Family provides a foundation like nothing else can, especially when you know you have the right person for you. You're going to have some good times and some bad times. That's just the nature of a relationship. It demands so much of each of you every day. But as a couple, as a family unit, you've got to fight through those moments and hold on to everything you have together. I'm very fortunate in that sense.

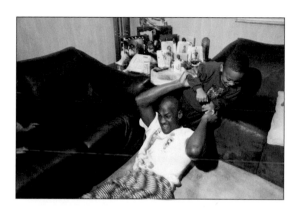

IF MY BOYS WANT TO PLAY BASKETBALL, THAT'S FINE. I'd rather they played another sport, but if that's what they want to do, then I'll support them. I'm never going to steer them away from something they want to do. I will try to give them as many options as possible. That's all I can do. They have to make their own decisions. But whatever they do, I'll support them.

I am afraid for them, though. I'm aware of how hard it will be for them to be the sons of a star athlete. The expectations will be different for them. Not just in sports either. They will be expected to have nice clothes or to get a Porsche when they turn 16 because everyone will know that their father has money.

They will have to deal with all kinds of peer pressures and I know that a lot of it won't be any fun for my kids. I've thought a lot about the pressure they might feel. You have to explain certain things to them early and instill a solid sense of values so that they will be able to deal with those things later on.

I will always have a very open relationship with them and let them know that they can come and talk to me about anything. I want them to know that if I can help them get through anything that I will be there. I want to be a friend and a brother as much as I am a parent. I also know I have to try to understand what they are going through at that time. Maybe you have to think back and remember what you were thinking when you were a kid at the same age. But then, as a parent, give them the guidance they need to get through whatever problem they might be facing. I know it's not easy being a kid these days.

HOUSEWORK? MECHANICAL WORK? I WAS LAZY AS A KID. My father was unbelievable. Nothing went to the shop. If the toaster broke, he would fix it. If the car needed the oil changed or the engine needed to be taken out for new pistons, he would do it. My brother Larry started to pick up on that attitude and my oldest brother Ronnie had already picked it up. So my father was kind of waiting for me. He would always try to lead me out there to the garage to help them out.

One time he asked me to pass him the 9/16ths wrench. I said, 'What the hell is a 9/16ths wrench?' That would make him so mad because I wasn't following in his footsteps and becoming a mechanically inclined person. I'm the type of guy that if something happens to my car, come pick it up. It's broken. Change a tire? I'm calling Triple A. I don't have the kind of understanding about those things that my father and brothers have. And that drove my father nuts. He would tell me, 'Go on in there with the women. Go in there and learn how to do the dishes.' I'd say, 'Sure.' I don't have a problem with that. I'm not going to get my nails dirty. I don't know anything about any 9/16ths wrench. But I can wash dishes. At least I know how to do that.

I'VE GIVEN MY BOYS DIFFERENT THINGS LIKE GOLF CLUBS, BASEBALL BATS, FOOTBALLS, THINGS LIKE THAT. But they are still basketball crazy. It doesn't matter whether it's on those little baskets at home or on the higher ones where the Bulls practice — they love it. I did a commercial where at the end a kid makes a basket and as the ball goes through the net he says, 'Yes!' They do the exact same thing. It's wild.

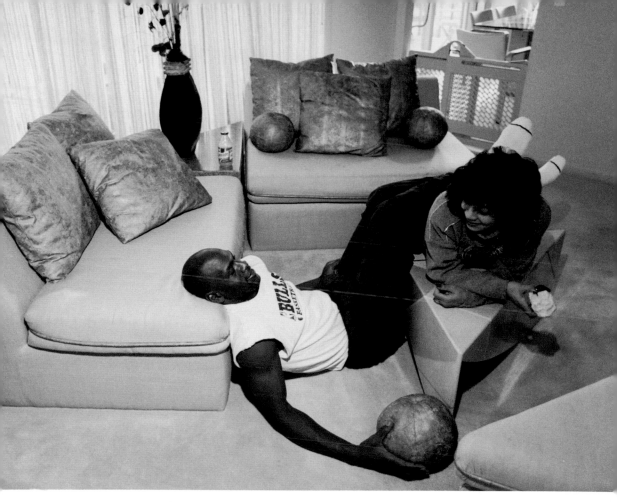

I really enjoy being married. But it was a tough situation for me. It was like I had a split personality when Juanita and I got married. Everyone projected me to be older and more mature and I tried to live that way. Yet I was only 24, 25 years old. I was caught in between and it was hard for me to know who I was at that time.

On the other hand, Juanita is four years older than me and she had gone through that period. So when we met, she was already at a more mature stage while I was still in a more adventurous stage. For us to get along and make it, I had to come up to her level.

And I'm happy I made the decision to do that. Marriage has given me a whole new perspective on life, particularly life after basketball. We have a great relationship. She's like my mother and I mean that in the best possible sense. When I've got problems, even basketball problems, I can talk to her. I know she's going to have a biased opinion when it comes to the game, but we can talk about anything.

My kids love the water, but not me. I've had too many bad experiences. When I was seven years old, I was out playing in the ocean with a friend. We were out swimming near Wilmington, N.C. where I grew up. I couldn't swim so we were just fooling around, body surfing and riding the waves. Then a big wave came in and the undertow grabbed his feet. Actually, he had stepped into a hole and I was standing right next to him. The next thing I knew he was going under and he put the death lock on me. I was so scared and I was going under. He was trying to take me with him. He needed help, but I couldn't help him because I wasn't a swimmer. I did all I could to keep him from going out to sea, to keep both of us from going out. I finally got free and made it back to shore, but he never made it. He drowned. That's why I don't fool around with water.

But that was just one incident. When I was 12, I remember almost drowning myself. We had just won the state baseball championship and we were celebrating. Everybody was hopping in the pool and swimming. Me, I couldn't swim but I wanted to celebrate. So I put myself on one of those beach balls and just kind of rode the water. We were at King's Mountain, N.C.

Anyway, one kid did a cannonball. You know where you grab your legs and tuck your knees to your chest to make a big splash? Well, he jumped in and knocked that beach ball out from under me. And I just kept going down. I went down once, twice, and the third time, one of my teammates grabbed my hand and put me on the side of the pool. I wouldn't have made it otherwise.

Then, I had a girlfriend at the University of North Carolina. Well, she went home one weekend, Memorial Day weekend, and there had been a bad storm in Wilmington with lots of heavy rain. She was walking in knee-deep water and the current knocked her down. She couldn't get back up and the current was so fast that the water took her out to sea and she drowned. In knee-deep water!

If that wasn't enough, North Carolina had this rule where you couldn't graduate unless you passed a swimming test. So, like a fool, I'm thinking I'm the greatest athlete around and I decide I'm going to try to pass the swimming test, knowing I can't swim. You had to swim down the length of the pool, swim back and then tread water. So I'm swimming down, at least what I call swimming, and as I was coming back, I went down twice. They threw me that big ole tire to grab onto. You couldn't see anything but a blur grabbing for that tire.

I know that's kind of embarrassing, but I don't give a damn. Give me my drawers back and let me out of here. I have a terrible phobia about the water. And I'm not embarrassed to say that. Everybody's afraid of something, so just don't ask me to go near any water.

I DO MISS ALL THE TIME THAT I'M NOT THERE. They change so much. My little girl, Jasmine, was starting to crawl by the end of the playoffs. I had missed the stages that led up to her actually trying to crawl. I missed the whole stage where she started to stand up, where she tried to move but really couldn't get going. I missed all that.

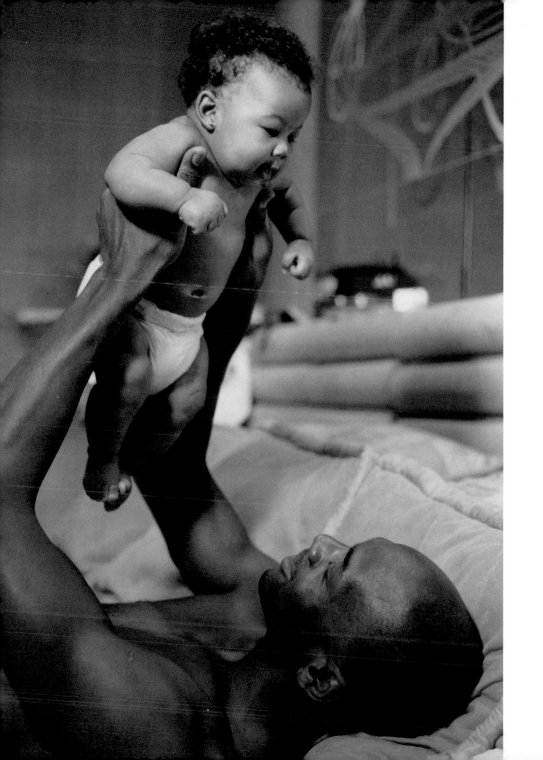

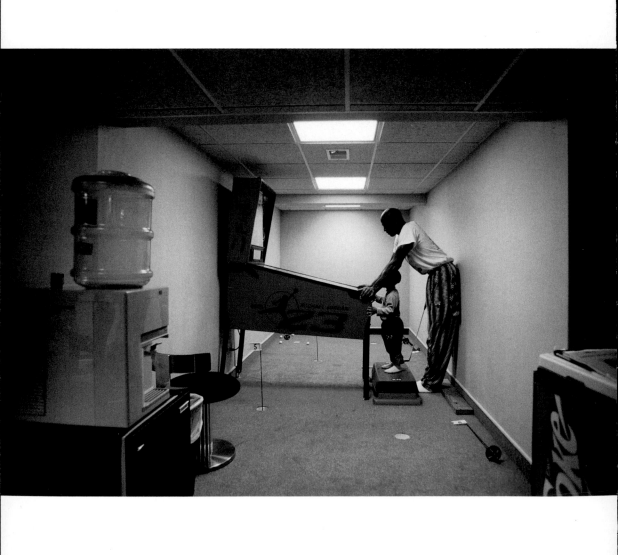

MY SONS ARE TOTALLY DIFFERENT. Jeffrey is very outgoing. He's a people person. He'll sit and talk to anybody. You can kid around with him, play with him, whatever. Marcus is totally different because he's so independent. Unless you're a woman. If you're a woman, Marcus will come up and kiss you all day. He loves women. He's a woman's man right now. I think he's going to be that way, too. Jeffrey's afraid of them a little bit, at least until he gets comfortable. Marcus is unbelievable. If there's a woman around, he'll go right up and lie down next to her. He's got all the moves of a playboy already.

I think they'll both end up being athletes. Jeffrey will probably be more of a baseball or basketball player. He has good eye-hand coordination and big hands. But Marcus, he has really big hands and he's so aggressive. I can't see Marcus doing anything but playing football. He'll be too big.

Growing up I was a lot like Marcus. I was independent, always in trouble. If I didn't like somebody I wouldn't talk to them. I did what I wanted to do. That's Marcus. I think he's going to be tough because I was tough. I did things just to be different.

My ninth grade year I was in trouble every day. I got suspended on the first day of school. We had a rule that you couldn't leave campus, but I left anyway to go get a soda. I came back and the principal was standing there waiting for me. He suspended me for three days. Other times, I told the teacher to get lost. All kinds of stuff. That was my bad year. I was really bad. That's when *Roots* was just coming out and I was very rebellious. I was in trouble at home all the time. I fought with my sisters and brothers. I didn't like them because I felt like they were more loved than I was at that particular time.

I felt like I was the black sheep of the family. I didn't want to work. I didn't want money. All I wanted to do was play basketball or other sports. My mother forced me to take a job at a hotel doing maintenance work. I did all kinds of odd jobs like cleaning cigarette butts off the sidewalk. I was 15 or 16. It was during that period that I told my mom, 'I'm not going to get out there and sweep up the sidewalk and have all my boys come by and see me sweeping up like some janitor.' So I quit that job after a week. My mother was so mad. She said, 'Fine. Now you're not going to have any money to buy anything.' I thought, 'Fine. Now I can stay here and play basketball all day long.'

My sisters and brothers all had jobs. Ronnie drove the school bus. My sisters, Delores and Roslyn, worked at Hardee's or McDonald's. My brother Larry had his job driving the school bus and doing ROTC. Me? I would go home and mess around. I didn't want to do my homework. But my mother would make me do it. I couldn't get away from that. I was about a C+ or B- student up until that time.

But once I saw that I had the ability to be a good student, I became a very good student. I think I left high school with a 3.2 or 3.3 grade point average. I could have gone to North Carolina on an academic scholarship even without basketball. I was good at math and I was good at all my precollege courses. I took chemistry, calculus, all those classes. I came to realize how important school was to my future. That's something I want my children to understand.

I WAS ALWAYS THE TYPE OF GUY THAT WENT FOR THE HOME RUN.

I'M ABLE TO RELAX IN MY OWN WAY WITH MY FRIENDS, PLAYING CARDS OR PLAYING GOLF. It may be on the run, but I am able to relax. It's just that my way of relaxing probably wouldn't be considered relaxing by most people. I can't stay home and do nothing unless I'm tired. I can't stay in bed all day or just lie around the house. As long as I have energy, and I almost always have energy, I have to be doing something. Most of the time I prefer anything with competition involved. I don't care what it is — ping pong, golf, cards, shooting pool or playing basketball. It doesn't matter.

I love to compete and it isn't the money. I just love the competition. I like the challenge. I could play you for a dollar. But like I've said before, if I'm going to play then I'm going to play to win. That's enjoyable to me. That's fun.

I've never known competing to be a major problem. I don't believe I've ever heard of Competitors Anonymous. I know I'm not at a point in my life where I'm jeopardizing my family's standard of living with any gambling that I might do. I am nowhere near that. It's just a game, a game that I want to win. If I'm playing you in golf, for example, I don't have to play for anything. We can play for pride. That's enough. But I am going to try to beat you.

Other than sports, about the only thing I did growing up was play the trumpet when I was in the seventh and eighth grade. But you had to practice so much, and with me playing basketball, which, like band, was right after school, I had to make a decision. I think I made the right one. I love music but I don't think I'd like to hear myself play.

As far as business goes, I won't do anything on Sunday. I mean, even the Lord rested on Sunday. And doing endorsements is work. A lot of work. I enjoy some of the people and some of the relationships I have. But I have a group of people that I've signed up with for ten years or more — Wilson Sporting Goods, Hanes, Gatorade, Nike and Upper Deck — and that's who I'll do most of my business with in the future.

THE COURSE SHOOTS PAR EVERY DAY. That's the challenge with golf. And that's enough to drive me. That's also why I think I will be able to play professionally when I'm finished with basketball.

It will be different for me. It really will be a hobby, a very difficult and demanding hobby, but a hobby nonetheless. If I win, great. But I am going to try to play it professionally. I've never really worked at the game to this point. I only play about three months out of the year. That's why I think once I put my mind to it, I'll be able to compete at that level.

Plus, there are a lot of comparisons between golf and basketball. You have to use your mind, you have to prepare yourself mentally to play both games. You have to know when to be aggressive, when not to be aggressive. You have to understand the game before you can play the game. Basketball is no different.

I don't have a problem being humble either. It won't bother me starting at the bottom. I want to go through the whole process just like every other golfer who has had to work his way up. I wouldn't want anything given to me because then I'd be judged differently. I'd rather go through every stage just like everyone else. If I fail, then I fail. If I don't, then at least everyone will know that I made it on my own.

My plan is to take five years. I'll spend all that time learning every phase of the game. I'll practice with the right people, the best people. And I'll spend the necessary time practicing. If I can't do it after five years of intense training, then I can't do it. But I think I'll be able to. I won't be like most of the professionals on the PGA Tour. I won't be playing for a living. I'll be playing for the challenge. These guys play for the competition, but they're also playing for the money. I won't need the money. It will be a whole different attitude.

PEOPLE ASKED ME HOW I FELT AFTER THAT GUY STABBED
MONICA SELES. That kind of thing scares me but not to the
point where I've got security guards and bodyguards
around me all the time. If they want to get to me, they
can get to me. I don't want to live as a captive. I don't
want to be afraid of leaving my room on the road or
walking out my front door at home.

I want to play golf, for example. My life is comfortable
and I'm not willing to change because of some threats.
I do get threats. Now if I feel that the threat is real, that's
a different story.

A crazy fan? I can't identify with that. I'm aware that
they exist. I can't identify with whomever he or she
might be, but I'm aware that there are some jerks out
there that might try to do something.

When I was 12 years old, my brother Larry and I were the starting back-court in Pee Wee League. He was the defensive guy and I was the scorer. So I hit the winning basket and as we were riding home my father said, 'Larry, that was great defense you played.' I'm saying, 'Damn. I stole the ball and scored the winning layup.' In my mind I'm thinking that evidently my father didn't see what I did, so I have to show him.

But it's funny how you look at those situations and all the steps that led to your competitive attitude. Then you look back trying to find the source and you find it goes back to that one game or Little League. I was always the type of guy that went for the home run. Larry would go for the base hit. My father would always say, 'That's a great attitude to have, going for the base hit.' I'd say, 'Why go for the base hit when you can go for all four bases?' That was my logic. And that's how I played.

One thing I would like to do, either when I'm through playing or one of these summers when I do have free time, is play baseball. I haven't totally dismissed that yet. I'd really like to go to a training camp, which I can't do because it's in the middle of our season, and give it a shot. I wouldn't have to stay there long, but I'd really like to see if I could do it. I'm serious. I'd love to try. It's an unfulfilled part of my life because I was never able to do what I wanted to do in college.

I was actually a better baseball player than I was a basketball player when I was growing up. I always thought I'd be a professional baseball player. Then I started to grow and I got more interested in basketball. But I still kept playing baseball.

In fact, I was going to go to South Carolina, Clemson or Mississippi State after high school because they all wanted me to play baseball and basketball. I was going to South Carolina until I visited North Carolina and fell in love with the place. But I'm serious about trying baseball. Bo Jackson did it. He's inspired me.

I THINK IT'S BEEN A COMBINATION OF MY FATHER'S AND MOTHER'S PERSONALITIES THAT HAS ALLOWED ME TO BECOME THE PERSON I AM. They are so different in some ways yet they are so similar. My father is a people person. He can talk to someone for five hours and have any conversation you could imagine.

My mother is opposite in a sense. She knows how to play the game. That's where I learned how to mingle with CEOs and at the same time still have a good relationship with inner-city kids. That's the game of life, being flexible and open enough to move between different circles of people. My mother has always been more of the business side of the family. She had a kind of 'Get up and go get it' attitude. My father was more like 'I don't need all those fancy clothes. I can wear these dungarees.'

In some ways, I'm the same way. I'm happy with my contract with the Bulls. I signed the contract and I'll always be loyal to that deal. I'm not going to go in and complain about it or whine to the media about how I should make more money. I gave my word and my word is my bond. Now, if you want to give me a raise, I'll accept it.

My mother is totally opposite. She would say, 'I think you should get more money, son. I think you should hold out and get what you're worth.' That's the business side of my mother. And I have some of that, too.

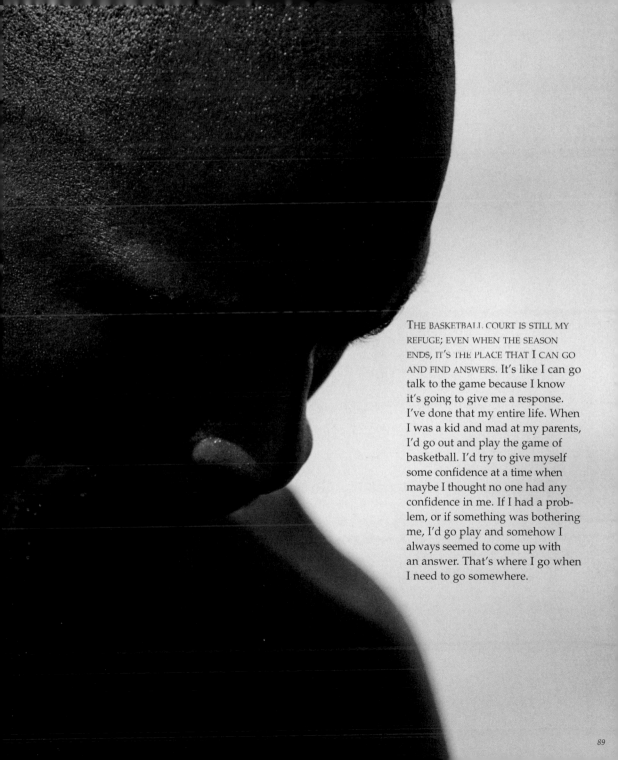

THE BASKETBALL COURT IS STILL MY REFUGE; EVEN WHEN THE SEASON ENDS, IT'S THE PLACE THAT I CAN GO AND FIND ANSWERS. It's like I can go talk to the game because I know it's going to give me a response. I've done that my entire life. When I was a kid and mad at my parents, I'd go out and play the game of basketball. I'd try to give myself some confidence at a time when maybe I thought no one had any confidence in me. If I had a problem, or if something was bothering me, I'd go play and somehow I always seemed to come up with an answer. That's where I go when I need to go somewhere.

THE CHALLENGE WAS RIGHT IN FRONT OF ME. I CAN RESPOND TO THAT.

38
PLR F PTS
Coca-Cola
Winston
GRANT
54
KONCAK
32
31
diet Coke
BULLS
57
HAWKS
38
TIME OUT
Hawks
SEARS

THE PLAYOFFS ARE TOTALLY DIFFERENT FROM THE REGULAR SEASON. For us, the regular season is even tougher in some ways, especially the 1992-93 season. You always have that feeling that you can turn it on in the playoffs. You always feel like you have that ace in the hole and that it's something you can fall back on regardless of what happens during the regular season.

But sometimes you can start to skip steps mentally. Then the next thing you know, you're physically skipping steps and you start asking yourself, 'Why are we going through another 82-game season when we know the rewards are in the playoffs?' During our first two title runs, we would focus game-to-game. We wanted to have the best record in the Eastern Conference. Bang, we got it. The best record in the entire league. Bang, we got that too.

But then we started skipping steps and saying to ourselves, 'Let's just get to the playoffs. Let's just get back to playing for a world championship.' That's hard to do. We had won championships when nobody thought we could, so that had been a little bit of a challenge in itself. Now, after you've done that, you start to get a little full of yourself and the next thing you know you're backing into bad situations. You might get out of one, two or even three of those, but eventually that becomes your downfall. You're relying on your ability to overcome your bad habits.

So it's hard to get motivated when you know that the rewards, everything you really want, come at the end of the playoffs. About the only thing you can get during the regular season is home-court advantage and, as we showed, that's not always a guarantee of anything.

The biggest problem we had, in a sense, was repetition. Anytime you have to repeat a past success it seems like you lose a little of that initial edge. It's easier to say, 'That's all right. I've got one ring,' or 'I've got two rings. Who cares about another one really?' That kind of thinking started to creep in and sometimes we didn't have the drive necessary to elevate our game to the next level. Other teams, particularly during the regular season, sensed that weakness and they attacked. The next thing you know, we're in a dogfight.

We had to get our backs against the wall, like we did against New York in the Eastern Conference finals, before we realized it's not going to be that easy and that we had to lift our game or else there wouldn't be any more games to play.

If we could have skipped the regular season and still qualified for the playoffs, even if we had the worst playoff position, everyone would have said, 'Fine.' It wouldn't have mattered because there had been so little motivation to excel, or to lift our game every night. That's what the playoffs are for.

PHOENIX WAS NO PROBLEM, AT LEAST COMPARED TO NEW
YORK. Charles (Barkley) was talking all his stuff because
he thought he could carry the load. But I've been there,
man, and that's a tough load to carry, especially the first
time. When the pressure's on and you need a basket, but
you're too tired to take the shot and when you do it
ends up short, you know you'll be answering to the
newspapers tomorrow. I think the load, the pressure of
being in the Finals and all the hype that surrounds

every game, was bigger than he thought it would be
because he hadn't been through it before.

Charles used all his methods to try to get his team fired
up. He tried to carry them. He pushed and pulled and
talked about the championship being part of the Suns'
'destiny.' I told him, 'Don't give me that destiny crap.
It's destined that you're all going to have a long summer.'

But I was glad when it was over. Winning a third straight
championship was the hardest thing I've ever done on
the basketball court.

EVERYONE HAS A THEORY AS TO WHY I WALKED AWAY. What they don't know is that I had been thinking about it for two years. Even after we won the first championship, I thought about not coming back the next season. No one believes that, but it's true.

Halfway through the 1992-93 season, I knew it would be my last. I had known for awhile that I wanted to go and do something else. And I had committed to the idea long before the playoffs started. I knew it was time to move on. I needed another challenge. I needed to do other things. Once I made that decision, I just tried to finish the job which was to win a third straight championship. So when we won, I knew I wasn't coming back. I was just waiting for the right time to make the announcement.

I had become tired of the regular season. The practices weren't the same. I was losing the excitement I had for practice, for that competition every day. Right then I knew I needed to do something else with my life. I didn't know whether Jerry Reinsdorf was going to give me an opportunity to play baseball, although I had been throwing little comments his way during that last season. Every chance I had I'd mention it to him. But I don't think he ever really took me seriously until I asked him.

My father was the only person who knew during the season I was retiring. My wife knew, or at least had a feeling, that I was getting tired of the grind. The whole thing had become all-consuming. Basketball, for the first time, had become a job. Sometimes I felt like I was just going through the motions.

Then to go out on top like that—the script couldn't have been written any better. By winning three in a row, I felt like it kind of distinguished me from Larry and Magic. There were no questions left. The only questions that could have been asked of Michael Jordan were no longer basketball-related. Everything seeped into the personal side and I found myself trying to defend myself more and more. I thought, 'I haven't done anything wrong. I'm just trying to be a human.' But it seemed like some people wanted me to be more than that, more than a human being. The burden had become too tiresome. I needed a vacation from that arena. I needed another look on life.

I CAN'T ACCEPT NOT TRYING.

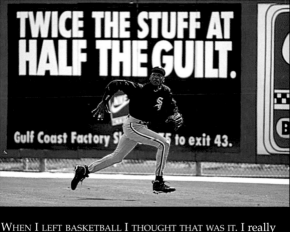

WHEN I LEFT BASKETBALL I THOUGHT THAT WAS IT. I really never thought I'd play again professionally. I had always wanted to play baseball, but I also knew I had to wait for the right time. Even after I retired, I had to give myself some time to make sure that my pursuing that dream was the right thing to do because I'd be walking into a situation similar to the one I left.

What people didn't know was how I felt about the game and whether I would take baseball seriously. They didn't realize that baseball was my first love. So they started attacking me saying, 'He doesn't have the skills, he's going to embarrass himself, he's going to embarrass the image or the legend that he built.' They started looking at my playing baseball so negatively instead of thinking, 'Hey, this is kind of neat. Here's a guy on top of the world and now he's going to try something that he hasn't done in 14 years. That's fun.' It should have been looked at as fun.

Instead they also made it seem like I was going to embarrass the sport by coming out and falling on my face and not really working hard. But they didn't understand me as a person. If they did, they would have known that I have never gone into anything halfheartedly. If I'm going to be a participant, then I'm going to put my heart into it. I'm going to do the work and I'm going to be focused so that I won't be embarrassed. And that's what I did.

But those minor leaguers,
most of whom will never reach
the major leagues, reminded me
of that process. They had a hold
of that dream and they weren't
about to let it go. If you told
those guys to swim a garbage
river and they would smell like
garbage when they got out, but
they would make the major
leagues, boy, they would dive
in headfirst. That's how much
they believed in their dreams.
Here I had fulfilled all my
dreams and was trying to do
something else, and these guys
didn't have a thing in the world.
They got $16 per diem. Those
guys would walk a mile to save
a dollar. They had so much
motivation.

I had reached my dreams, I had
it all. But these guys, they didn't
have anything and they were
the happiest guys in the world.
That kind of thing was infec-
tious. It made me think.

I loved the whole experience.
And I always felt like I fit right
in, even in those minor league
hotels. We'd drive all night, get
in at 10 a.m., sleep two hours
and go play baseball. We'd stay
at the La Quinta Inn, or the
Ramada Inn or the Holiday Inn.
No room service. And in some
places, the restaurant would
close between 2 and 4 p.m.

But I loved being around those
guys. I miss them more now
than ever. They were so pure,
their dreams so real. They were
fun to be around. And they all
wanted to play basketball. They
always wanted to see if I could
still play so we used to play on
Sundays. They always treated
me like one of the guys. They'd
slap me on the head just like
everyone else. There were
things like that I hadn't experi-
enced in so long outside of my
brothers or close friends. Those
guys were just fun and yet we
really didn't do a whole lot. I
ended up playing a lot of card
games and crossword puzzles.

I was usually the last guy to
leave the clubhouse. I would
stay back and talk to the
coaches, play Yahtzee. We'd
just hang around. By the time I
was ready to leave the park, it
would usually be two hours
after the game. I really miss
that atmosphere.

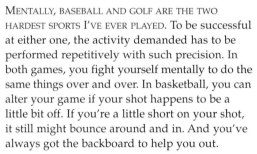

Mentally, baseball and golf are the two hardest sports I've ever played. To be successful at either one, the activity demanded has to be performed repetitively with such precision. In both games, you fight yourself mentally to do the same things over and over. In basketball, you can alter your game if your shot happens to be a little bit off. If you're a little short on your shot, it still might bounce around and in. And you've always got the backboard to help you out.

Baseball's different. I got really down midway through the 1994 season and almost came home. We were in Memphis playing against our big rival at the time. Here I am, a fierce competitor, and I just wasn't pulling my weight. I struck out four times and the last time the bases were loaded with two outs in the top of the ninth. All I needed was a hit, and we'd go up one. He gave me three straight sliders and I looked like a damn windmill. That was the lowest point.

I came into the locker room and talked to Terry Francona, the manager. It was about an hour after the game and I was still in my uniform when I walked into his office. I said, 'Let me ask you something. And I want you to be frank with me. Am I doing the right thing? Did I make the right decision coming down here and playing baseball? Because if not, then I'm wasting my time and yours. And I don't feel comfortable doing that, because right now I'm really ready to go home.' I talked to him and Barney, who was the hitting instructor. They told me about their experiences in minor league baseball and how everyone, everyone, goes through a period where it's just not clicking.

They said, 'Don't think you're the only one going through this because every player has gone through it. You just have to work your way out of this phase. It's not something that's just happened to you.' So I took that advice for what it was worth and I started working extra hard. I changed my swing to where it made me feel more natural and things started turning around. From that point on, I batted over .300.

became a lot bigger physically during my time in baseball. About all I did was lift weights. I was trying to get up to 228 pounds. My legs, my wrists, my forearms, that's where I was trying to add strength and size. I probably took 500 swings a day during the season, so physically I had to build myself up to take that abuse. I was using a completely different muscle group compared to what my body had been used to. But all the work paid off.

weighed 218 when I decided to return to basketball. And it wasn't a fat 218. My legs were bigger, I felt stronger. But I didn't have any wind. I was bigger and stronger than I had ever been but I couldn't run a mile. So I had to cut down fast. I was so afraid of being that big and trying to move like I knew I had to move on the basketball court. I was afraid the extra weight would put too much strain on my knees. In the 18 months away from the game, I hadn't had any signs of tendonitis, which is very common in basketball players. So that was my primary concern when I came back.

I THINK I COULD HAVE MADE IT TO THE MAJOR LEAGUES BUT I'LL NEVER KNOW. The only thing I know for sure is that I had a great time. I was exposed to a lot of things I never knew about the game of baseball. And I found out those guys are great athletes. They may not look like basketball players, but they are athletes. They have a specialty, an art. And it isn't something easily obtained. It's a talent you have to do everything you can to enhance.

I'd probably still be playing if there hadn't been a baseball strike. It just got to be so political and all I wanted was to play the game. I didn't want to get caught up in making money for the owners, or not making money for the players. Instead of focusing on what I was trying to achieve in baseball, so many problems were revolving around me because of my basketball career. I never wanted to be in that position. Ultimately, I chose to walk away. But I walked away with a better appreciation for the game and, as it turned out, I had a period of time away from basketball. I didn't know I was getting a break from basketball and it wasn't planned. It just worked out that way.

THE PRESSURE PUT ON ME, LIKE A LOT OF MINOR LEAGUERS DURING THE STRIKE, WAS INDIRECT. But there never should have been any pressure because I had always let everyone know exactly where I stood on the whole issue. I never wanted to be pushed and pulled into the middle of it all. That's what was disappointing. It wasn't fair to me and it certainly wasn't fair to the other minor leaguers. When I realized I was being put in the middle I couldn't trust anyone to give me an honest answer about the real reason I was there.

They had other interests, another agenda. I was there to play the game and find whether I had the skills to do that. I wasn't there to become a bargaining chip for one side or the other. So I walked away gracefully. But I also walked away disappointed and angry, not for myself, but for all those minor league players who I admired for their perseverance and passion. They were being used, as I would have been, and they didn't have a choice. They were caught. I could walk away with my dreams and not worry about feeding my kids and my family. They had to make a choice, and whichever one they made had a penalty attached to it.

If they played, the players would call them scabs. If they didn't play, the owners might say, 'Well, we don't know if you'll have a job when the strike is over.' And that was a travesty. Here are guys holding onto the little bit of hope they have for this game, yet it all came down to making a moral judgement that didn't have a morally correct answer. In professional sports, athletes are taught to make the best moral judgement for themselves and their careers. These guys were trying to do that and yet they were going to be penalized no matter what decision they made.

There were so many confused guys coming to me and asking what they should do. It made me feel really awkward. If it had been basketball, then I would have been able to give them a better sense of what to do. But this was baseball, a game in which I had been looking to them for guidance. I felt like an older brother at the time. All I told them was, 'Look inside yourself and see what your ultimate goal is and evaluate your ability to get there. Now, if you're good enough to play in the majors, no matter what decision you make, you're going to get there. They can't take your skill level away from you. If you're good enough then you're going to shine.'

That was the simplest way I could put it. I couldn't tell them to go this way because then they were going to have concerns about that direction. It was a tough decision and I was glad I didn't have to make it. They had to look at their lives and answer some questions. Do you need the money? Do you have other ways of making a living? Most of them just had to do what they had to do to earn a living.

But no one stood up for them. No one. What was wrong was the major leaguers were asking the minor leaguers to stand up for them. But if those minor league guys were kicked out of camp and not invited back when the strike was over, who was going to stand there and strike for those players until they got their jobs back? So why ask them to stand up for you when you're not going to stand up for them? That's not fair. They got dumped on. These were 18, 19 and 20 year old guys, some of them 26 or 27, and all they were trying to do was hold onto a dream.

I'M BACK!

AFTER BASEBALL I HAD NO PLANS TO PLAY BASKETBALL AGAIN. I just thought, 'I'm going to go home, start playing golf, hang around and do nothing.'

I went to practice, which was something I had done before. I had an open mind, but I really wasn't thinking about coming back. Then I talked to Phil. I always felt that if there was anybody I really let down when I left, it was Phil and the coaches, because I never let them know ahead of time I was going to retire. They never had a chance to prepare. That's one reason I would stop in and talk to him even when I was playing baseball. I'd ask him if he was still hanging in there, whether or not he was going to quit, just to kind of see where his mind was.

At that first practice a lot of the players started talking about me playing. Tex (Winter) was always after me. He'd say, 'You know you could come back and play and practices will be different. You still have some good years in you.' That was Tex just always nipping at me. Still, I wasn't really thinking about it until the players, Scottie, B.J., guys I knew, said they really wanted me to come back.

That's when I fixed on the idea that these guys needed me to come back and help them win. And that's what initiated the thoughts, the idea that those guys needed me to come back. I kind of missed them anyway.

I always wanted to play just the playoffs. So as it turned out, everything came together at the perfect time. Once I decided, I didn't want to dwell on the decision because I knew if I really thought about it, I'd come up with all the good reasons why I shouldn't come back. I easily could have said, 'No, my pride won't let me. I walked away on top. Why would I want to come back and open up that can of worms?'

But what made me get past those thoughts was the idea that there was a need and that I could actually help the situation. That's when I started thinking about it seriously.

I WORE NO. 45 UNTIL MY BROTHER
LARRY AND I WERE ON THE SAME TEAM
IN HIGH SCHOOL. Since he wore the
same number, I had to change mine.
So I figured I would cut it in half, but
you couldn't wear 22 ¹/₂ so I settled
on No. 23. I wore No. 23 from that
point on.

I KNEW I WOULD HAVE TO MAKE ADJUSTMENTS WHEN I CAME BACK. I had to learn to play with certain players just like they had to learn to play with me. But I also had to adjust to playing in a new arena. I never liked the United Center, which was fine, because I never thought I'd play there. I always thought that building was all about business instead of having a true home court, a kind of place other teams don't like. But now they come into the United Center and opposing teams have to love it, because for them the Stadium was a joke. But the Stadium was home to us.

Opposing teams wanted to get out of there as soon as possible because the floor was cold and maybe they had a couple showers that didn't work. But now if it's cold, they can just turn up the thermometer over on the wall. I mean, the amenities are unbelievable. But I had fixed in my mind the fact that I was never going to play

there. Now that I am playing there, mentally I've got to accept that, and I've got to become comfortable with that building just like I was with the Stadium.

I knew every little thing about the Stadium, every nook and cranny. I knew the people who worked there, the guys that picked up the floor and put it down every day, the ladies I'd walk past. There was one lady that would always say, 'Good Day' or 'Good Morning' every time I came through. Those are the things that make the home court an advantage.

This new building has a lot of people I've never seen before. So before I can do well there, I've got to know those people. It's like moving into a new house. If you don't know the maid or you don't know the housekeeper, you just don't feel comfortable around that person, even if it is your house. So that's what I have to do.

I DIDN'T HAVE ANY SENSE OF FEEL WHEN I CAME BACK. Even that game-winning shot against Atlanta didn't feel right. It must have been fate because I didn't feel very good about the shot when I let it go. It was like I somehow willed it into the basket.

In fact, I really didn't feel good until the New York game. That game showed why basketball is so unique for me. You can play horribly with half the world looking. But when the whole world is watching, you play like a champ. I couldn't have written a better storyline. We were going into New York against our old nemesis, a team we had always gone to war against. I hadn't had a great game, yet everyone was waiting for an outburst. And there you go. I couldn't miss a shot. If anything, I went into that game with lower expectations. I was less confident than I have ever been going into a game. The next thing you know, everything clicks and I make the first four jump shots. That night I didn't feel any different than I did the night before. It's so peculiar.

What I think that game did was let my teammates know that I was still capable of scoring 55 points against the so-called 'best defense' in the NBA. Maybe it also gave them a little extra confidence because maybe they thought, 'What happens when he gets his rhythm and his timing back?'

I SPEND A LOT MORE TIME WITH MY CHILDREN NOW AND THAT'S NOT GOING TO CHANGE. I've got a set routine where I get up and take my kids to school, go to practice and then come home and play with them. If I have to do a commercial, I try to make sure I come back home in time to play before I put them in bed.

I was so wrapped up in my job, which is what basketball had become when I retired, that everything else had become secondary. I had always told them, 'Your daddy's going to play a game.' But toward the end, it became, 'Hey, I've got to go off to my job and I'll be home after work.'

But it's different now. If you want me to do a commercial, well, let me see if I can fit it in around my family. Before I log in a commercial date, let's see if Jeffrey's got a basketball game or whether Marcus has hockey practice. I want to take some of the burden of raising our children off my wife because I think it has to be a dual responsibility. I know she has had to give up things she's wanted to do. Now, I want to be there. So in that sense my life is more normal now. If we win another championship, I'm not sure how long my life will remain normal, but I want to try to keep outside demands from seeping in. I want to keep everything in perspective and do what I enjoy first, which is being with my children, and do what I *have* to do second. I'll play through the end of my contract and see where everything stands.

My kids do like to watch Bulls games, though. Will they sit around and watch another game with me? No. But I'll have to watch *Lion King* again when the game's over.

THE LAST THREE YEARS I PLAYED WE EXPECTED TO BE CHAMPIONS. This time people didn't know what we could do in the playoffs. Do you know how mentally draining that can be for an opponent? Charlotte knew it was playing the Chicago Bulls but those guys didn't know what I was capable of doing. Will he come out and score 55? Will he come out and do this? Will he come out and do that? No matter how much you watched us on television, it wasn't the same.

But once the games started, they had to deal with all those unknowns. They hadn't seen me for 82 games. They knew I was coming, but they didn't know how I was coming. I might have come by land, I might have come by air. They didn't know if I'd changed. They didn't know if I was the same. They might have known how to deal with Scottie, but what about both of us at the same time? That's one reason I was confident going into the playoffs.

We also had four guys that had won three championships in a row. Outside of Houston, there wasn't another championship team out there. Horace Grant won with us, but Orlando hadn't won anything until they beat Boston in the first round. We knew the mental preparation necessary going into playoff games and we knew what to expect. I thought that gave us an advantage going into the Orlando series.

Before, we had a swagger about what we could do. And we backed it up. But this team only went 12-4 with Michael Jordan. So what can they do in the playoffs? There were a lot questions when playoffs started, but no one had answers. There was a lot of speculation but no one knew. That was the element of surprise. To a certain extent, I think that will be true in the future as well.

BEYOND THE CAMERA: A LIVING INDEX

OBSERVATIONS BY WALTER IOOSS, JR.

COVER
This was taken on the roof of the Mayfair Hotel in Miami in March. I asked the lifeguard to hold an umbrella over Michael and I put a large white umbrella on the ground to bounce the light back into his face. The wall was perfect.

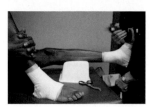

PAGE 17
I took a shot of Michael's feet and he said, "This is only for the book." His wife Juanita said, "I can't believe he let you take that shot." Michael's toes take a beating.

PAGE 12
Michael has a gym area in the basement of his house. He said he started lifting after the all-star game so he would be strong for the playoffs. Once again it shows the dedication of the guy. I'd call him at 9:30 p.m. and he'd be down lifting weights.

PAGES 24-25
Part of Michael's pregame ritual is to put resin on his hands and slap them together in front of announcer Johnny Kerr's face. Johnny can be seen here protecting himself.

PAGE 14
Michael had told me that he doesn't like to talk while driving to a game. I had one question and said I wouldn't talk anymore out of respect for his pregame solitude. He said, "I don't initiate conversation, but I'll answer questions."

PAGES 28-29
Compared to other players, Michael doesn't take that much of a beating. He's like Ali. He floats.

PAGE 16
Stacey King was doing an imitation of a white television personality. He was very funny and Michael, along with the other players, just sat and laughed. The team had just arrived for a game at Miami.

PAGE 31
I remember when I showed these to Michael. He said, "Look at my feet." It's the perfect defensive posture. Bring this picture to any coach and they'll tell you. It's perfect. He loved this picture.

PAGES 32-33
This used to be his claim to fame, driving to the basket. I'm sure he's lost something over the years, but his first step might still be the fastest because everyone is so concerned with his jump shot now.

PAGES 38-39
This was during the Knicks series. I had never seen Scottie, or any player for that matter, touch Michael's head like that. This was just one of those strange moments of fellowship among two players trying to hold on during a tough series. They were having a hard time against the Knicks.

PAGE 34
This is one of my favorite shots. Every time I show this to Michael I tell him, 'This is the one Rony Seikaly blocked.' Michael says, "No way. Seikaly never blocked that shot. You're crazy." He's probably right. He remembers everything that happens in a game.

PAGE 42
It's like a long-distance runner that crosses the line and passes out. He plays all out as long as he can. But then he wants to get off the court because he knows his next ordeal is the media. He's winding down, but he's still in the game.

PAGE 37
You rarely see dunks anymore, particularly the acrobatic dunks he did when he was younger. A lot of people miss him flying, but he has to conserve his energy. And he doesn't need to fly because he can hit jumpers all day.

PAGE 44
He had just scored more than 50 points and they had lost. You could see that he was getting irritated because he was being grilled about how the team had lost. The whole team had sort of evacuated the room and he was left all alone to handle the media.

PAGES 46-47
This is the essence of Michael in the locker room after a game. He's the first one in the shower and the first one dressed because he always wants to be completely dressed whenever the media comes in.

PAGE 51
They have food and drinks the moment they get onto the plane. Michael has his own compartment. It's four seats, two across from each other. It's very comfortable.

PAGE 49
At Chicago Stadium, off-duty police provide security for Michael and his family. From the moment he arrives to the moment he leaves, they are around. They watch Juanita and his children wherever they go.

PAGE 53
I was amazed at his dedication. After we arrived in Orlando, he started getting treatment on his sprained ankle. Every 90 seconds he would switch from hot to cold water. Then he took ultrasound treatments. He did this all through the next day. Finally he put on shoes to see if he could walk. That night he scored 36 points.

PAGE 50
This shows how different Michael is compared to other athletes. His corner room in the Plaza overlooked Central Park. It seemed like such an unusual picture, this contrast between legends, old world and present day. Ahmad Rashad and Quinn Buckner were with Michael almost all the time during the playoffs.

PAGES 54-55
He didn't sleep well the night before. So when I knocked on his door about noon, Michael just walked back and flopped onto the bed with his favorite friend on the road, the remote control. He started going in and out of sleep while I was shooting. Off the court, he's always horizontal.

PAGE 57
I was worried that Jasmine would be cranky and hard to pose. But it was Marcus who became restless. This was the only good shot out of 36.

PAGE 66
Look at the form. It's like the original Nike poster. They look just like Michael. It struck me how aggressively they were dunking. One night the kids announced the starting lineup, just like Chicago Stadium. They love B.J. Armstrong.

PAGE 62
They are two different kids. Jeffrey is a huggable guy while Marcus has this serious look like he's going to run through a wall. But they long for more time with Michael, there's no doubt about that.

PAGES 68-69
I wonder as I look back if Michael thought the tub was too deep. That's what was going through my mind. I know he doesn't like the water.

PAGES 64-65
All through the house, including the kitchen, you see Nike, McDonald's and Gatorade products.

PAGE 71
This was special because Michael really loves his little daughter. He's always talking about Jazzy. When he got on the bed with Jasmine, he knew the camera was there but you could feel the love between them.

PAGE 72
This is the only pinball machine of its kind. The game is extremely noisy, but Marcus loves it. Jeffrey, though, he won't go near it. It's right on Michael's putting green in the basement.

PAGES 78-79
Michael's serious on the golf course. He doesn't want to lose at anything. He has fun. He jokes. But he doesn't slow down. He wants to beat everybody and he wants to do it fast so he can play as many holes as possible.

PAGE 75
The flash would go off occasionally and I remember Michael kept saying, "You sure you know what you're doing?" But if there is one thing that goes with Michael, it's that car. Not everybody can wear a car like that.

PAGE 81
Juanita was pregnant with Jasmine and Michael called home to see how she felt. He had been playing well. But after the phone call he bogeyed the next two holes. Smiling, he said, "Never call your wife from the golf course."

PAGE 77
We had come in off the golf course in Orlando. Michael went right to the pool table. Once he started playing, I knew this wasn't my game.

PAGE 83
This was shot in the concierge lounge in Orlando. Near the end of the shoot, four women walked by and recognized him. They asked him what he did on the road. Michael said he stayed in his room. "Don't you like people?" the woman asked. "Not anymore," Michael replied. He really is a prisoner of his fame.

PAGE 85

I think he was as big a star at the all-star game as anyone actually there to play the game. He wore his uniform all day. He really enjoyed that day. He'd love to play baseball, but I can't see him languishing in the minor leagues very long.

PAGE 9?

They ne___ say a word before they go onto the court. It's like this is the time when they are at their office. It's time to work.

PAGE 86

Twice a week, Tuesday and Friday, Michael shaves his head.

PAGE 94

After the game ended, Michael was heading off the floor. For a split second he forgot what he was doing. His normal reaction was to get off the court as soon as possible. Moments later, he had to run back onto the court to do the McDonald's commercial.

PAGES 88-89

I've had the camera in his face and he never alters what he's doing. Whenever you photograph somebody, unless it's a model, they alter their pose. Michael never moves. I think he's used to eyes constantly on him. It's like I'm invisible.

PAGE 96

One thing that struck me in the playoffs was how much communication was going on between Phil and Michael. It was like he was a coach on the floor. They never talked as much during the season as they did throughout the playoffs.

PAGE 97
Michael and Magic. This was in Los Angeles and it was the first time since the Olympics that they had seen each other. I remember Michael saying that he had told Magic to slow down and take it easy now that he was out of the limelight.

PAGE 116
The trainer's room at the United Center is the largest I've ever seen in sports. Everyone had been taped and there Michael sat, the biggest star in the game alone in this huge room.

PAGE 101
This was Michael's first game in Sarasota. All the media had shown up and Michael knew they were there to see him fail. But he still looked graceful. And I'll say one thing—no one ever looked better in a baseball uniform.

PAGE 121
After the New York game in Chicago, Juanita brought the kids to see Michael. What struck me was the sheer joy in his face when he saw them. At that moment, it was like he forgot about everything. His face just lit up when he took Jasmine in his arms.

PAGE 113
Michael, Scottie and B.J. hanging around the Orlando locker room before Game 1 of the Eastern Conference semifinals. Michael was doing a crossword puzzle. It seemed like just another game.

PAGE 123
When you're around Michael a lot, you start to believe that he will always find a way to beat an opponent. It doesn't matter who is on the court and which team Michael's playing against. I know people have said he looks different than before, but his moves all looked the same to me.

WALTER IOOSS, JR. has been associated with *Sports Illustrated* for more than 25 years. His memorable images have appeared on more than 200 covers of the magazine, an achievement unequaled by any other sports photo-journalist. His award-winning work has been exhibited in prestigious museums throughout the country including National Geographic Society's Explorer's Hall in Washington, D.C., the Museum of Photographic Art in San Diego, the Museum of Science and Industry in Chicago, and the International Center of Photography in New York City. He has published two books of his greatest photographs, *Football* and *Baseball*.

MARK VANCIL, developer and coordinator of the *Rare Air* project, worked for ten years as an award-winning writer/reporter for the *Chicago Sun-Times*, *Minneapolis-Star Tribune*, and *The National Sports Daily*. Mark's relationship with Michael Jordan dates back to 1984, Jordan's rookie season with the Chicago Bulls. In addition to covering Michael on a daily basis for the *Sun-Times* and *The National*, Mark and Michael have collaborated on a number of magazine articles, including the *Playboy* interview (May, 1992). Currently, Mark provides creative direction and project coordination for a number of corporate clients and professional organizations.

McMILLAN ASSOCIATES, a leading Chicago-based design firm, has been in the business of creating award-winning visual communications and printed publications for more than eight years. With an international roster of clients, McMillan Associates has a reputation for innovative approaches and solutions to communication design.